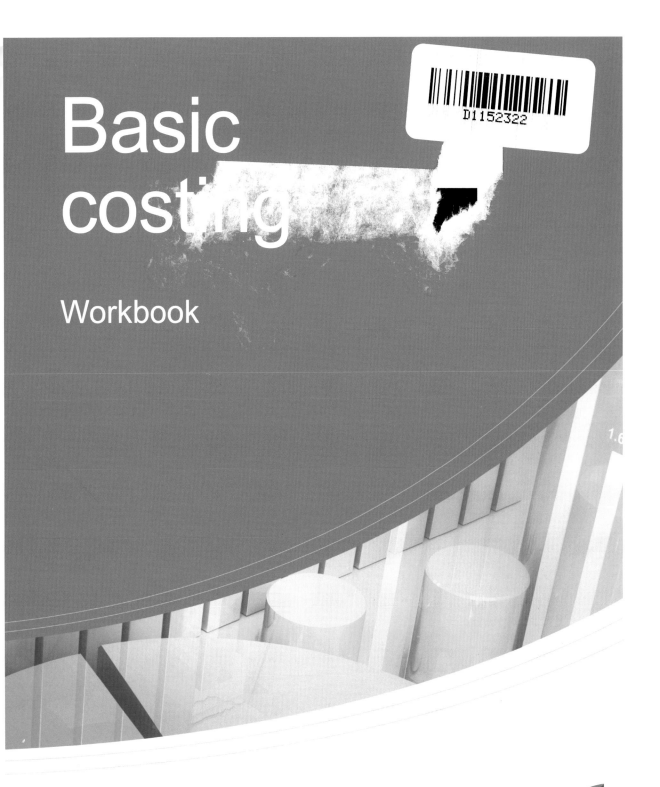

Basic
costing

Workbook

Aubrey Penning

osborne
BOOKS

Published by Osborne Books Limited
Unit 1B Everoak Estate
Bromyard Road
Worcester WR2 5HP
Tel 01905 748071
Email books@osbornebooks.co.uk
Website www.osbornebooks.co.uk

Design by Laura Ingham
Cover and page design image © Istockphoto.com/Petrovich9

Printed and bound by CPI Group (UK) Ltd., Croydon, CR0 4YY

British Library Cataloguing in Publication Data
A catalogue record for this book is available from the British Library

ISBN 978 1905777 747

Contents

Chapter activities

Chapter activities – answers

Practice assessments

Practice assessments – answers

Acknowledgements

The publisher wishes to thank the following for their help with the reading and production of the book: Maz Loton, Jon Moore and Cathy Turner. Thanks are also due to Jo Osborne for her technical editorial work and to Laura Ingham for her designs for this series.

The publisher is indebted to the Association of Accounting Technicians for its help and advice to our author and editors during the preparation of this text.

Author

Aubrey Penning has many years experience of teaching accountancy on a variety of courses in Worcester and Gwent. He is a Certified Accountant, and before his move into full-time teaching he worked for the health service, a housing association and a chemical supplier. Until recently he was the AAT course coordinator at Worcester College of Technology, specialising in the areas of management accounting and taxation.

Introduction

what this book covers

This book has been written specifically to cover the Learning Area 'Basic Costing' which combines two QCF Units in the AAT Level 2 Certificate in Accounting:

- Basic principles of costing
- Provide basic cost and revenue information

what this book contains

This book is set out in two sections:

- **Chapter activities** which provide extra practice material in addition to the activities included in the Osborne Books Tutorial text. Answers to the Chapter activities are set out in this book.

- **Practice assessments** are included to prepare the student for the Computer Based Assessments. They are based directly on the structure, style and content of the sample assessment material provided by the AAT at www.aat.org.uk. Suggested answers to the Practice assessments are set out in this book.

online support from Osborne Books

This book is supported by practice material available at www.osbornebooks.co.uk

This material is available to tutors – and to students at their discretion – in two forms:

- A **Tutor Zone** which is available to tutors who have adopted the Osborne Books texts. This area of the website provides extra assessment practice material (plus answers) in addition to the activities included in this Workbook text.

- **Online learning** – online practice questions designed to familiarise students with the style of the AAT Computer Based Assessments.

further information

If you want to know more about our products, please visit www.osbornebooks.co.uk, email books@osbornebooks.co.uk or telephone Osborne Books Customer Services on 01905 748071.

Chapter activities

1 Chapter activities
The costing system

1.1 The table below lists some of the characteristics of financial accounting and management accounting systems. Indicate two characteristics for each system by putting a tick in the relevant column of the table below.

✔

Characteristic	Financial Accounting	Management Accounting
Records transactions that have already happened		
Provides accounts that comply with legal requirements		
Looks in detail at future costs and income of products and services		
May use estimates where these are the most suitable form of information		

1.2 Hideaway Ltd is a manufacturer of garden sheds.

Classify the following costs into materials, labour or overheads by putting a tick in the relevant column of the table below.

✔

Cost	Materials	Labour	Overheads
Wood used to make sheds			
Insurance of factory			
Wages of employees who cut window glass to size			
Wages of carpenter who assembles shed panels			

1.3 Hideaway Ltd is a manufacturer of garden sheds.

Classify the following costs by nature (direct or indirect) by putting a tick in the relevant column of the table below.

Cost	Direct	Indirect
Wood used to make sheds		
Insurance of factory		
Wages of employees who cut window glass to size		
Wages of carpenter who assembles shed panels		

1.4 Dave's Plaice is a take away fish and chip shop.

Classify the following costs by putting a tick in the relevant column of the table below.

Cost	Direct Materials	Direct Labour	Indirect Costs
Potatoes used to make chips			
Maintenance of cooking equipment			
Wages of employees who fry fish and chips			
Gas to cook fish and chips			

1.5 Trendy Limited manufactures clothing.

Classify the following costs by function (production, administration, or selling and distribution) by putting a tick in the relevant column of the table below.

Cost	Production	Administration	Selling and Distribution
Purchases of cloth			
Salespeople's salaries			
Insurance of office building			
Salaries of sewing machinists			

2 Chapter activities
Cost centres and cost behaviour

2.1   Falcon Ltd is a manufacturer of toys.

Classify the following costs by their behaviour (fixed, variable, or semi-variable) by putting a tick in the relevant column of the table below.

✔

Cost	Fixed	Variable	Semi-Variable
Managers' salaries			
Production workers paid a fixed wage plus a production-based bonus			
Packaging materials for finished toys			
Factory insurance			

2.2   Omega Ltd, a manufacturer of furniture, uses a numerical coding structure based on one profit centre and three cost centres as outlined below. Each code has a sub-code so each transaction will be coded as ***/***

Profit/Cost Centre	Code	Sub-classification	Sub-code
Sales	100	UK Sales	100
		Overseas Sales	200
Production	200	Direct Cost	100
		Indirect Cost	200
Administration	300	Indirect Cost	200
Selling and Distribution	400	Indirect Cost	200

Code the following income and expense transactions, which have been extracted from purchase invoices, sales invoices and payroll, using the table below.

Transaction	Code
Factory lighting	
Warehouse repairs	
Sales to Newcastle, UK	
Sales to India	
Materials to upholster chairs	
Factory maintenance wages	

2.3 Smooth Running Limited operates a garage that repairs and maintains cars. It uses a coding system for its costs (materials, labour or overheads) and then further classifies each cost by nature (direct or indirect cost) as below. So, for example, the code for direct materials is A100.

Element of Cost	Code	Nature of Cost	Code
Materials	A	Direct	100
		Indirect	200
Labour	B	Direct	100
		Indirect	200
Overheads	C	Direct	100
		Indirect	200

Code the following costs, extracted from invoices and payroll, using the table below.

Cost	Code
Wages of trainee mechanic	
Wages of receptionist	
Oil used for car servicing	
Depreciation of electronic tuning equipment used for car servicing	
Replacement parts used for car repairs	

2.4 Complete the table below showing fixed costs, variable costs, total costs and unit cost at the different levels of production. Calculate unit cost to the nearest penny where appropriate.

Units	Fixed Costs	Variable Costs	Total Costs	Unit Cost
1,000	£20,000	£5,000	£25,000	£25.00
2,000	£	£	£	£
3,000	£	£	£	£
4,000	£	£	£	£

2.5 Omega Ltd is costing a single product which has the following cost details:

Variable Costs per unit

Materials	£5
Labour	£4
Total Fixed Overheads	£90,000

Complete the following total cost and unit cost table for a production level of 15,000 units.

	Total Cost	Unit Cost
Materials	£	£
Labour	£	£
Fixed Overheads	£	£
Total	£	£

3 Chapter activities
Inventory valuation and the manufacturing account

3.1 Identify the correct inventory (stock) valuation method from the characteristic given by putting a tick in the relevant column of the table below.

✔

Characteristic	FIFO	LIFO	AVCO
Issues of inventory are valued at the oldest purchase cost			
Issues of inventory are valued at the average of the cost of purchases			
Inventory balance is valued at the most recent purchase cost			

3.2 Identify whether the following statements about inventory (stock) valuation are true or false by putting a tick in the relevant column of the table below.

✔

	True	False
FIFO costs issues of inventory at the average purchase price		
AVCO costs issues of inventory at the oldest purchase price		
LIFO costs issues of inventory at the most recent purchase price		
LIFO values inventory balance at the most recent purchase price		
FIFO values inventory balance at the most recent purchase price		
AVCO values inventory balance at the latest purchase price		

3.3 Omega Ltd has the following movements in a certain type of inventory into and out of its stores for the month of March:

Date	Receipts		Issues	
	Units	Cost	Units	Cost
March 5	300	£900		
March 8	200	£800		
March 12	500	£2,200		
March 18			600	
March 25	400	£2,000		

Complete the table below for the issue and closing inventory values.

Method	Value of Issue on 18 March	Inventory at 31 March
FIFO	£	£
LIFO	£	£
AVCO	£	£

3.4 Place the following headings and amounts into the correct format of a manufacturing account on the right side of the table, making sure that the arithmetic of your account is accurate. The first entry has been made for you.

	£		£
Prime Cost	73,000	Opening inventory of raw materials	10,000
Opening inventory of raw materials	10,000		
Closing inventory of work in progress	19,000		
Direct labour	30,000		
Opening inventory of work in progress	10,000		
Closing inventory of finished goods	14,000		
Closing inventory of raw materials	11,000		
Cost of goods sold	96,000		
Raw materials used in manufacture	43,000		
Purchases of raw materials	44,000		
Factory cost of goods manufactured	85,000		
Opening inventory of finished goods	25,000		
Manufacturing overheads	21,000		
Factory cost	94,000		

3.5 Magnum Ltd has the following movements in a certain type of inventory into and out of its stores for the month of September:

Date	Receipts		Issues	
	Units	Cost	Units	Cost
September 5	400	£800		
September 8	250	£450		
September 12			300	
September 18	500	£1,200		
September 25	400	£1,000		

Complete the table below for the issue and closing inventory values.

Calculate final values to nearest £.

Method	Value of Issue on Sept 12	Inventory at 30 Sept
FIFO	£	£
LIFO	£	£
AVCO	£	£

Chapter activities
4 Labour costs

4.1 Identify the labour payment method by putting a tick in the relevant column of the table below.

✔

Payment Method	Time-rate	Piecework	Time-rate plus bonus
Labour is paid based entirely on the production level achieved			
Labour is paid according to hours worked, plus an extra amount if an agreed level of output is exceeded			
Labour is paid only according to hours worked			

4.2 Greville Ltd pays a time-rate of £12 per hour to its direct labour for a standard 38 hour week. Any of the labour force working in excess of 38 hours is paid an overtime rate of £18 per hour.

Calculate the gross wage for the week for the two workers in the table below.

Worker	Hours Worked	Basic Wage	Overtime	Gross Wage
A Summer	38 hours	£	£	£
S Cambridge	43 hours	£	£	£

4.3   Omega Ltd uses a piecework method to pay labour in one of its factories. The rate used is £1.30 per unit produced.

Calculate the gross wage for the week for the two workers in the table below.

Worker	Units Produced in Week	Gross Wage
V Singh	320 units	£
A Evans	390 units	£

4.4   Omega uses a time-rate method with bonus to pay its direct labour in one of its factories. The time-rate used is £10 per hour and a worker is expected to produce 20 units an hour. Anything over this and the worker is paid a bonus of £0.25 per unit.

Calculate the gross wage for the week including bonus for the three workers in the table below.

Worker	Hours Worked	Units Produced	Basic Wage	Bonus	Gross Wage
A Samuel	35	650			
J McGovern	35	775			
M Schaeffer	35	705			

4.5   Identify the following statements as true or false by putting a tick in the relevant column of the table below.

✔

	True	False
Indirect labour costs can be identified with the goods being made or the service being produced		
Direct labour costs never alter when the level of activity changes		
The classification of labour costs into direct and indirect does not depend on the method of calculation of the pay		

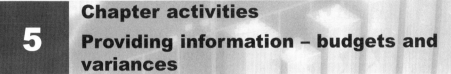

Chapter activities

5 Providing information – budgets and variances

5.1 Identify the following statements as being true or false by putting a tick in the relevant column of the table below.

✔

	True	False
A budget is a financial plan for an organisation that is prepared in advance		
If actual costs are more than budgeted costs the result is a favourable variance		

5.2 Greville Ltd has produced a performance report detailing budgeted and actual cost for last month.

Calculate the amount of the variance for each cost type and then determine whether it is adverse or favourable by putting a tick in the relevant column of the table below.

Cost Type	Budget £	Actual £	Variance	Adverse	Favourable
Direct Materials	93,500	94,200	£		
Direct Labour	48,700	47,800	£		
Production Overheads	28,000	31,200	£		
Administration Overheads	28,900	27,700	£		
Selling and Distribution Overheads	23,800	23,100	£		

5.3 The following performance report for last month has been produced for Greville Ltd as summarised in the table below. Any variance in excess of 4% of budget is thought to be significant and should be reported to the relevant manager for review and appropriate action.

Examine the variances in the table below and indicate whether they are significant or not significant by putting a tick in the relevant column.

✔

Cost Type	Budget £	Variance	Adverse/ Favourable	Significant	Not Significant
Direct Materials	93,500	£700	A		
Direct Labour	48,700	£900	F		
Production Overheads	28,000	£3,200	A		
Administration Overheads	28,900	£1,200	F		
Selling and Distribution Overheads	23,800	£700	F		

5.4 It was noted from the performance report for Greville Ltd for an earlier month that the following cost variances were significant:

- Direct Materials Cost

- Selling and Distribution Overheads

These variances needed to be reported to the relevant managers for review and appropriate action if required.

Select from the following list a relevant manager for each significant variance to whom the performance report should be sent:

- Human Resources (HR) Manager
- Sales Manager
- Managing Director
- Purchasing Manager

- Production Manager
- Training Manager
- Distribution Manager

Variance	Manager
Direct Materials Cost	
Selling and Distribution Overheads	

5.5 Locale Ltd makes a single product and for a production level of 18,000 units has the following cost details:

Direct Materials   6,000 kilos   at £27 per kilo

Direct Labour   9,000 hours   at £10 an hour

Overheads   £36,000

Complete the table below to show the unit cost at the production level of 18,000 units.

Element	Unit Cost
Materials	£
Labour	£
Overheads	£
Total	£

Answers to chapter activities

1 Chapter activities – answers
The costing system

1.1

Characteristic	Financial Accounting	Management Accounting
Records transactions that have already happened	✔	
Provides accounts that comply with legal requirements	✔	
Looks in detail at future costs and income of products and services		✔
May use estimates where these are the most suitable form of information		✔

1.2

Cost	Materials	Labour	Overheads
Wood used to make sheds	✔		
Insurance of factory			✔
Wages of employees who cut window glass to size		✔	
Wages of carpenter who assembles shed panels		✔	

1.3

Cost	Direct	Indirect
Wood used to make sheds	✔	
Insurance of factory		✔
Wages of employees who cut window glass to size	✔	
Wages of carpenter who assembles shed panels	✔	

1.4

Cost	Direct Materials	Direct Labour	Indirect Costs
Potatoes used to make chips	✔		
Maintenance of cooking equipment			✔
Wages of employees who fry fish and chips		✔	
Gas to cook fish and chips			✔

1.5

Cost	Production	Administration	Selling and Distribution
Purchases of cloth	✔		
Salespeople's salaries			✔
Insurance of office building		✔	
Salaries of sewing machinists	✔		

2

Chapter activities – answers
Cost centres and cost behaviour

2.1

Cost	Fixed	Variable	Semi-Variable
Managers' salaries	✔		
Production workers paid a fixed wage plus a production-based bonus			✔
Packaging materials for finished toys		✔	
Factory insurance	✔		

2.2

Transaction	Code
Factory lighting	200/200
Warehouse repairs	400/200
Sales to Newcastle, UK	100/100
Sales to India	100/200
Materials to upholster chairs	200/100
Factory maintenance wages	200/200

2.3

Cost	Code
Wages of trainee mechanic	B100
Wages of receptionist	B200
Oil used for car servicing	A100
Depreciation of electronic tuning equipment used for car servicing	C200
Replacement parts used for car repairs	A100

2.4

Units	Fixed Costs	Variable Costs	Total Costs	Unit Cost
1,000	£20,000	£5,000	£25,000	£25.00
2,000	£20,000	£10,000	£30,000	£15.00
3,000	£20,000	£15,000	£35,000	£11.67
4,000	£20,000	£20,000	£40,000	£10.00

2.5

	Total Cost	Unit Cost
Materials	£75,000	£5.00
Labour	£60,000	£4.00
Fixed Overheads	£90,000	£6.00
Total	£225,000	£15.00

Chapter activities – answers
3 Inventory valuation and the manufacturing account

3.1

Characteristic	FIFO	LIFO	AVCO
Issues of inventory are valued at the oldest purchase cost	✔		
Issues of inventory are valued at the average of the cost of purchases			✔
Inventory balance is valued at the most recent purchase cost	✔		

3.2

	True	False
FIFO costs issues of inventory at the average purchase price		✔
AVCO costs issues of inventory at the oldest purchase price		✔
LIFO costs issues of inventory at the most recent purchase price	✔	
LIFO values inventory balance at the most recent purchase price		✔
FIFO values inventory balance at the most recent purchase price	✔	
AVCO values inventory balance at the latest purchase price		✔

3.3

Method	Value of Issue on 18 March	Inventory at 31 March
FIFO	£2,140	£3,760
LIFO	£2,600	£3,300
AVCO	£2,340	£3,560

3.4

	£		£
Prime Cost	73,000	Opening inventory of raw materials	10,000
Opening inventory of raw materials	10,000	Purchases of raw materials	44,000
Closing inventory of work in progress	19,000	Closing inventory of raw materials	11,000
Direct labour	30,000	Raw materials used in manufacture	43,000
Opening inventory of work in progress	10,000	Direct labour	30,000
Closing inventory of finished goods	14,000	Prime Cost	73,000
Closing inventory of raw materials	11,000	Manufacturing overheads	21,000
Cost of goods sold	96,000	Factory cost	94,000
Raw materials used in manufacture	43,000	Opening inventory of work in progress	10,000
Purchases of raw materials	44,000	Closing inventory of work in progress	19,000
Factory cost of goods manufactured	85,000	Factory cost of goods manufactured	85,000
Opening inventory of finished goods	25,000	Opening inventory of finished goods	25,000
Manufacturing overheads	21,000	Closing inventory of finished goods	14,000
Factory cost	94,000	Cost of goods sold	96,000

3.5

Method	Value of Issue on Sept 12	Inventory at 30 Sept
FIFO	£600	£2,850
LIFO	£550	£2,900
AVCO	£577	£2,873

Chapter activities – answers

Labour costs

4.1

Payment Method	Time-rate	Piecework	Time-rate plus bonus
Labour is paid based entirely on the production level achieved		✔	
Labour is paid according to hours worked, plus an extra amount if an agreed level of output is exceeded			✔
Labour is paid only according to hours worked	✔		

4.2

Worker	Hours Worked	Basic Wage	Overtime	Gross Wage
A Summer	38 hours	£456	£0	£456
S Cambridge	43 hours	£456	£90	£546

4.3

Worker	Units Produced in Week	Gross Wage
V Singh	320 units	£416.00
A Evans	390 units	£507.00

4.4

Worker	Hours Worked	Units Produced	Basic Wage	Bonus	Gross Wage
A Samuel	35	650	£350.00	£0.00	£350.00
J McGovern	35	775	£350.00	£18.75	£368.75
M Schaeffer	35	705	£350.00	£1.25	£351.25

4.5

	True	*False*
Indirect labour costs can be identified with the goods being made or the service being produced		✔
Direct labour costs never alter when the level of activity changes		✔
The classification of labour costs into direct and indirect does not depend on the method of calculation of the pay	✔	

Chapter activities – answers

5

Providing information – budgets and variances

5.1

	True	False
A budget is a financial plan for an organisation that is prepared in advance	✔	
If actual costs are more than budgeted costs the result is a favourable variance		✔

5.2

Cost Type	Budget £	Actual £	Variance	Adverse	Favourable
Direct Materials	93,500	94,200	£700	✔	
Direct Labour	48,700	47,800	£900		✔
Production Overheads	28,000	31,200	£3,200	✔	
Administration Overheads	28,900	27,700	£1,200		✔
Selling and Distribution Overheads	23,800	23,100	£700		✔

5.3

Cost Type	Budget £	Variance	Adverse/ Favourable	Significant	Not Significant
Direct Materials	93,500	£700	A		✔
Direct Labour	48,700	£900	F		✔
Production Overheads	28,000	£3,200	A	✔	
Administration Overheads	28,900	£1,200	F	✔	
Selling and Distribution Overheads	23,800	£700	F		✔

5.4

Variance	Manager
Direct Materials Cost	Production Manager or Purchasing Manager
Selling and Distribution Overheads	Sales Manager or Distribution Manager

5.5

Element	Unit Cost
Materials	£9.00
Labour	£5.00
Overheads	£2.00
Total	£16.00

Basic costing

Practice assessment 1

Time allowance: 2 hours

Section 1

Task 1.1

The table below lists some of the characteristics of financial accounting and management accounting systems.

Indicate which characteristics relate to each system by putting a tick in the relevant column of the table below.

Characteristic	Financial Accounting	Management Accounting
It is concerned with recording historic costs and revenues		
One of its main purposes is to provide information for annual financial statements		
It is accurate, with no use of estimates		
It looks forward to show what is likely to happen in the future		

Task 1.2

Octavia Ltd is a manufacturer of food products.

Classify the following costs into materials, labour or expenses by putting a tick in the relevant column of the table below.

✔

Cost	Materials	Labour	Overheads
Meat used in burgers			
Electricity used in factory			
Boxes to pack burgers			
Expenses of the sales manager			

Task 1.3

Citicars Ltd is in business as a taxi company.

Classify the following costs by nature (direct or indirect) by putting a tick in the relevant column of the table below.

✔

Cost	Direct	Indirect
Fuel for taxis		
Cost of servicing taxis		
Wages of taxi drivers		
Wages of reception staff		

Task 1.4

Granville Ltd manufactures mobile telephones from components.

Classify the following costs by function (production, administration, or selling and distribution) by putting a tick in the relevant column of the table below.

✔

Cost	Production	Administration	Selling and Distribution
Purchases of components for mobile telephones			
Commission paid to sales staff			
Rent of offices			
Wages of staff who assemble telephones			

Task 1.5

Fanfare Ltd is a manufacturer of musical instruments.

Classify the following costs by their behaviour (fixed, variable, or semi-variable) by putting a tick in the relevant column of the table below.

Cost	Fixed	Variable	Semi-Variable
Labour costs paid on a time basis			
Maintenance of website			
Power costs which include a standing charge			
Packing materials for completed instruments			

Task 1.6

Octavia Ltd, a manufacturer of food products, uses an alpha-numeric coding structure based on one profit centre and three cost centres as outlined below. Each code has a sub-code so each transaction will be coded as */***

Profit/Cost Centre	Code	Sub-classification	Sub-code
Sales	A	Restaurant Sales	100
		Supermarket Sales	200
Production	B	Direct Cost	100
		Indirect Cost	200
Administration	C	Direct Cost	100
		Indirect Cost	200
Selling and Distribution	D	Direct Cost	100
		Indirect Cost	200

Code the following revenue and expense transactions, which have been extracted from purchase invoices, sales invoices and payroll, using the table below.

Transaction	Code
Factory lighting	
Repairs to warehouse	
Meat for making burgers	
Sales to 'Kings Restaurant'	
Commission to sales staff	
Stationery for Administration	

Task 1.7

Citicars Limited operates a taxi business and uses a coding system for its costs of materials, labour or overheads, and then further classifies each cost by nature (direct or indirect cost) as below. So, for example, the code for direct materials is 50/100.

Cost	Code	Nature of Cost	Code
Materials	50	Direct	100
		Indirect	200
Labour	60	Direct	100
		Indirect	200
Overheads	70	Direct	100
		Indirect	200

Code the following costs, extracted from invoices and payroll, using the table below.

Cost	Code
Wages of taxi driver	
Vehicle insurance for taxis	
Wages of reception staff	
Fuel for taxis	
Office rent	

Task 1.8

Identify the following statements as either true or false by putting a tick in the relevant column of the table below.

	True	False
Variable costs change in proportion to changes in activity level		
Fixed costs remain unchanged when activity levels change		
Semi-variable costs change in proportion to changes in activity level		

Task 1.9

Classify the following costs as either fixed or variable by putting a tick in the relevant column of the table below.

✔

Cost	Fixed	Variable
Factory insurance		
Bonus for production staff paid per item produced		
Salaries of administration staff		
Repairs to a factory used for production		

Task 1.10

Complete the table below showing fixed costs, variable costs, total costs and unit cost at the different levels of production. Carry out unit cost calculations to the nearest penny.

Units	Fixed Costs	Variable Costs	Total Costs	Unit Cost
5,000	£25,000	£10,000	£35,000	£7.00
7,500	£	£	£	£
10,000	£	£	£	£
12,500	£	£	£	£

Task 1.11

Octavia Ltd is costing a single product which has the following cost details:

Variable Costs per unit

Materials	£8
Labour	£5
Total Fixed Overheads	£48,000

Complete the following total cost and unit cost table for a production level of 12,000 units.

	Total Cost	Unit Cost
Materials	£	£
Labour	£	£
Fixed Overheads	£	£
Total	£	£

Task 1.12

Eureka Ltd makes a single product and for a production level of 15,000 units has the following cost details:

Direct Materials	7,500 kilos	at £6 per kilo
Direct Labour	3,750 hours	at £11 an hour
Overheads		£60,000

Complete the table below to show the unit cost at the production level of 15,000 units.

Element	Unit Cost
Materials	£
Labour	£
Overheads	£
Total	£

Section 2

Task 2.1

Reorder the following costs into a manufacturing account format on the right side of the table below.

	£		£
Closing inventory of raw materials	10,000		
Direct labour	86,000		
Opening inventory of raw materials	9,000		
Closing inventory of finished goods	25,000		
Prime cost	133,000		
Factory cost of goods manufactured	195,000		
Cost of goods sold	200,000		
Factory cost	197,000		
Purchases of raw materials	48,000		
Opening inventory of work in progress	9,000		
Opening inventory of finished goods	30,000		
Manufacturing overheads	64,000		
Direct materials used	47,000		
Closing inventory of work in progress	11,000		

Task 2.2

Identify the correct inventory (stock) valuation method from the characteristic given by putting a tick in the relevant column of the table below.

✔

Characteristic	FIFO	LIFO	AVCO
Inventory is valued at the most recent purchase cost			
Issues are valued at the average of the cost of purchases			
Issues are valued at the oldest relevant purchase cost			

Task 2.3

Identify whether the following statements are true or false by putting a tick in the relevant column of the table below.

✔

	True	False
AVCO costs issues of inventory at the most recent purchase price		
FIFO costs issues of inventory at the oldest relevant purchase price		
LIFO costs issues of inventory at the oldest relevant purchase price		
FIFO values closing inventory at the most recent purchase price		
LIFO values closing inventory at the most recent purchase price		
AVCO values closing inventory at the most recent purchase price		

Task 2.4

Octavia Ltd has the following movements in a certain type of inventory (stock) into and out of its stores for the month of August:

Date	Receipts		Issues	
	Units	Cost	Units	Cost
August 12	100	£500		
August 14	350	£1,820		
August 17	400	£2,200		
August 18			700	
August 26	300	£1,680		

Complete the table below for the issue and closing inventory values.

Method	Value of Issue on 18 August	Inventory at 31 August
FIFO	£	£
LIFO	£	£
AVCO	£	£

Task 2.5

Identify the following statements as true or false by putting a tick in the relevant column of the table below.

✔

	True	False
Direct material costs cannot be identified with the goods being made or the service being produced		
Indirect costs never change when the level of activity alters		

Task 2.6

Identify the labour payment method by putting a tick in the relevant column of the table below.

✔

Payment Method	Time-rate	Piecework	Time-rate plus bonus
Labour is paid based entirely on attendance at the workplace			
Labour is paid a basic rate plus an extra amount if an agreed level of production is exceeded			
Labour is paid entirely according to each individual's output			

Task 2.7

Identify one feature for each labour payment method by putting a tick in the relevant column of the table below.

✔

Payment Method	Time-rate	Piecework	Time-rate plus bonus
Employee knows that pay will not fall below certain amount but will increase if output is high			
Employer and employee can both plan for regular expected amounts			
Employer's labour cost is entirely proportional to output			

Task 2.8

Granville Ltd pays a time-rate of £8 per hour to its direct labour for a standard 37 hour week. Any of the labour force working in excess of 37 hours is paid an overtime rate of £16 per hour.

Calculate the gross wage for the week for the two workers in the table below.

Worker	Hours Worked	Basic Wage	Overtime	Gross Wage
A Smith	37 hours	£	£	£
S Collins	41 hours	£	£	£

Task 2.9

Octavia Ltd uses a piecework method to pay labour in one of its factories. The rate used is £2.16 per unit produced.

Calculate the gross wage for the week for the two workers in the table below.

Worker	Units Produced in Week	Gross Wage
G Powell	109 units	£
S Singh	123 units	£

Task 2.10

Octavia Ltd uses a time-rate method with bonus to pay its direct labour in one of its factories. The time-rate used is £10 per hour and a worker is expected to produce 7 units an hour. Anything over this and the worker is paid a bonus of £0.50 per unit.

Calculate the gross wage for the week including bonus for the three workers in the table below.

Worker	Hours Worked	Units Produced	Basic Wage	Bonus	Gross Wage
A Weaton	40	250	£	£	£
J Davis	40	295	£	£	£
M Laston	40	280	£	£	£

Task 2.11

Identify the following statements as true or false by putting a tick in the relevant column of the table below.

✔

	True	False
A variance can be calculated as the difference between expected and actual income		
If expected income is greater than actual income the variance is favourable		

Task 2.12

Granville Ltd has produced a performance report detailing budgeted and actual cost for last month.

Calculate the amount of the variance for each cost type and then determine whether it is adverse or favourable by putting a tick in the relevant column of the table below.

.

Cost Type	Budget £	Actual £	Variance	Adverse	Favourable
Direct Materials	34,500	38,100	£		
Direct Labour	71,300	70,000	£		
Production Overheads	48,600	49,100	£		
Administration Overheads	89,400	84,900	£		
Selling and Distribution Overheads	51,200	51,900	£		

Task 2.13

The following performance report for this month has been produced for Granville Ltd as summarised in the table below. Any variance in excess of 8% of budget is thought to be significant and should be reported to the relevant manager for review and appropriate action.

Examine the variances in the table below and indicate whether they are significant or not significant by putting a tick in the relevant column.

Cost Type	Budget	Variance	Adverse/ Favourable	Significant	Not Significant
Direct Materials	£38,000	£3,300	A		
Direct Labour	£71,000	£8,000	A		
Production Overheads	£43,000	£4,200	F		
Administration Overheads	£50,000	£2,900	A		
Selling and Distribution Overheads	£47,000	£2,100	A		

Task 2.14

It was noted from the performance report for Granville Ltd for an earlier month that the following cost variances were significant:

• Production overheads cost

• Direct materials cost

These variances needed to be reported to the relevant managers for review and appropriate action if required.

Select from the following list a relevant manager for each significant variance to whom the performance report should be sent:

• Purchasing manager   • Production manager

• Accounts manager   • Administration manager

• Sales manager

Variance	Manager
Production overheads cost	
Direct materials cost	

Basic costing

Practice assessment 2

Time allowance: 2 hours

This Assessment is based on a sample assessment provided by the AAT and is reproduced here with their kind permission.

Section 1

Task 1.1

The table below lists some of the characteristics of financial accounting and management accounting systems.

Indicate which characteristics relate to each system by putting a tick in the relevant column of the table below.

Characteristic	Financial Accounting	Management Accounting
It is based on past events		
Its purpose is to provide information for managers		
It is based on future events		
It complies with company law and accounting rules		

Task 1.2

Olsen Ltd is a manufacturer of garden furniture.

Classify the following costs into materials, labour or expenses by putting a tick in the relevant column of the table below.

Cost	Materials	Labour	Overheads
Wood used in garden chairs			
Rent of factory			
Wages of carpenters in the cutting department			
Expenses of the office manager			

Task 1.3

Curly Ltd runs a hairdressing salon.

Classify the following costs by nature (direct or indirect) by putting a tick in the relevant column of the table below.

✔

Cost	Direct	Indirect
Conditioner used on hair		
Insurance of salon		
Wages of salon cleaner		
Wages of hair stylists		

Task 1.4

Greenside Ltd produces chocolate products.

Classify the following costs by function (production, administration, or selling and distribution) by putting a tick in the relevant column of the table below.

✔

Cost	Production	Administration	Selling and Distribution
Purchases of sugar			
Depreciation of sales department's motor vehicles			
Insurance of office furniture			
Salaries of production workers			

Task 1.5

Fairway Ltd is a manufacturer of clothes.

Classify the following costs by their behaviour (fixed, variable, or semi-variable) by putting a tick in the relevant column of the table below.

✔

Cost	Fixed	Variable	Semi-Variable
Material used in the production process			
Advertising budget for the year			
Electricity costs which include a standing charge			
Labour costs paid on a piecework basis			

Task 1.6

Olsen Ltd, a manufacturer of garden furniture, uses a numerical coding structure based on one profit centre and three cost centres as outlined below. Each code has a sub-code so each transaction will be coded as ***/***

Profit/Cost Centre	Code	Sub-classification	Sub-code
Sales	100	UK Sales	100
		Overseas Sales	200
Production	200	Direct Cost	100
		Indirect Cost	200
Administration	300	Direct Cost	100
		Indirect Cost	200
Selling and Distribution	400	Direct Cost	100
		Indirect Cost	200

Code the following revenue and expense transactions, which have been extracted from purchase invoices, sales invoices and payroll, using the table below.

Transaction	Code
Office heating	
Warehouse rent	
Sales to Oxford, UK	
Sales to North America	
Materials to stain tables	
Factory canteen wages	

Task 1.7

Curly Limited operates a hairdressing salon and uses a coding system for its costs of materials, labour or overheads and then further classifies each cost by nature (direct or indirect cost) as below. So, for example, the code for direct materials is A100.

Cost	Code	Nature of Cost	Code
Materials	A	Direct	100
		Indirect	200
Labour	B	Direct	100
		Indirect	200
Overheads	C	Direct	100
		Indirect	200

Code the following costs, extracted from invoices and payroll, using the table below.

Cost	Code
Salary of trainee hairdresser	
Legal costs to renew lease of salon	
Wages of salon cleaner	
Cleaning materials used by cleaner	
Colouring materials used on customers	

Task 1.8

Identify the following statements as either true or false by putting a tick in the relevant column of the table below.

✔

	True	False
Variable costs change directly with changes in activity		
Fixed costs change directly with changes in activity		
Semi-variable costs have a fixed and variable element		

Task 1.9

Classify the following costs as either fixed or variable by putting a tick in the relevant column of the table below.

✔

Cost	Fixed	Variable
Direct materials		
Wages of production workers paid using a time-rate method		
Wages of production workers paid by a piecework method		
Rent for a factory used for production		

Task 1.10

Complete the table below showing fixed costs, variable costs, total costs and unit cost at the different levels of production. Carry out unit cost calculations to the nearest penny.

Units	Fixed Costs	Variable Costs	Total Costs	Unit Cost
1,000	£12,000	£3,000	£15,000	£15.00
2,000	£	£	£	£
3,000	£	£	£	£
4,000	£	£	£	£

Task 1.11

Olsen Ltd is costing a single product which has the following cost details:

Variable Costs per unit

Materials	£2
Labour	£3
Total Fixed Costs	£80,000

Complete the following total cost and unit cost table for a production level of 20,000 units.

Element	Total Cost	Unit Cost
Materials	£	£
Labour	£	£
Fixed Costs	£	£
Total	£	£

Task 1.12

Ironside Ltd makes a single product and for a production level of 24,000 units has the following cost details:

Direct Materials	6,000 kilos	at £20 per kilo
Direct Labour	8,000 hours	at £12 an hour
Overheads		£48,000

Complete the table below to show the unit cost at the production level of 24,000 units.

Element	Unit Cost
Materials	£
Labour	£
Overheads	£
Total	£

Section 2

Task 2.1

Reorder the following costs into a manufacturing account format on the right side of the table below.

	£		£
Closing Inventory of Work in Progress	10,000		
Direct Labour	97,000		
Opening Inventory of Raw Materials	7,000		
Closing Inventory of Finished Goods	25,000		
Closing Inventory of Raw Materials	10,000		
Manufacturing Overheads	53,000		
Cost of goods sold	200,000		
Factory cost	197,000		
Purchases of Raw Materials	50,000		
Opening Inventory of Work in Progress	8,000		
Opening Inventory of Finished Goods	30,000		
Prime cost	144,000		
Direct materials used	47,000		
Factory cost of goods manufactured	195,000		

Task 2.2

Identify the correct inventory (stock) valuation method from the characteristic given by putting a tick in the relevant column of the table below.

✔

Characteristic	FIFO	LIFO	AVCO
Issues are valued at the most recent purchase cost			
Inventory is valued at the average of the cost of purchases			
Inventory is valued at the most recent purchase cost			

Task 2.3

Identify whether the following statements are true or false by putting a tick in the relevant column of the table below.

✔

	True	False
FIFO costs issues of inventory at the most recent purchase price		
AVCO costs issues of inventory at the oldest purchase price		
LIFO costs issues of inventory at the oldest purchase price		
FIFO values closing inventory at the most recent purchase price		
LIFO values closing inventory at the most recent purchase price		
AVCO values closing inventory at the latest purchase price		

Task 2.4

Olsen Ltd has the following movements in a certain type of inventory into and out of its stores for the month of March:

Date	Receipts		Issues	
	Units	Cost	Units	Cost
March 5	200	£600		
March 8	300	£1,200		
March 12	500	£2,500		
March 18			600	
March 25	400	£2,400		

Complete the table below for the issue and closing inventory values. Calculate closing values to the nearest £.

Method	Value of Issue on 18 March	Inventory at 31 March
FIFO	£	£
LIFO	£	£
AVCO	£	£

Task 2.5

Identify the following statements as true or false by putting a tick in the relevant column of the table below.

✔

	True	False
Direct labour costs can be identified with the goods being made or the service being produced		
Indirect costs vary directly with the level of activity		

Task 2.6

Identify the labour payment method by putting a tick in the relevant column of the table below.

Payment Method	Time-rate	Piecework	Time-rate plus bonus
Labour is paid based entirely on the production achieved			
Labour is paid extra if an agreed level of output is exceeded			
Labour is paid according to hours worked			

Task 2.7

Identify one feature for each labour payment method by putting a tick in the relevant column of the table below.

Payment Method	Time-rate	Piecework	Time-rate plus bonus
Assured level of remuneration for employee, but no reward for working efficiently			
Employee earnings depend entirely on output			
Assured level of remuneration and reward for working efficiently			

Task 2.8

Greenside Ltd pays a time-rate of £10 per hour to its direct labour for a standard 35 hour week. Any of the labour force working in excess of 35 hours is paid an overtime rate of £15 per hour.

Calculate the gross wage for the week for the two workers in the table below.

Worker	Hours Worked	Basic Wage	Overtime	Gross Wage
A Singh	35 hours	£	£	£
S Callaghan	40 hours	£	£	£

Task 2.9

Olsen Ltd uses a piecework method to pay labour in one of its factories. The rate used is 80p per unit produced.

Calculate the gross wage for the week for the two workers in the table below.

Worker	Units Produced in Week	Gross Wage
G Patel	300 units	£
A Jones	400 units	£

Task 2.10

Olsen Ltd uses a time-rate method with bonus to pay its direct labour in one of its factories. The time-rate used is £12 per hour and a worker is expected to produce 5 units an hour. Anything over this and the worker is paid a bonus of £1 per unit.

Calculate the gross wage for the week including bonus for the three workers in the table below.

Worker	Hours Worked	Units Produced	Basic Wage	Bonus	Gross Wage
A Smith	35	150	£	£	£
J O'Hara	35	175	£	£	£
M Stizgt	35	210	£	£	£

Task 2.11

Identify the following statements as true or false by putting a tick in the relevant column of the table below.

✔

	True	False
A variance is the difference between budgeted and actual cost		
A favourable variance means budgeted costs are greater than actual costs		

Task 2.12

Greenside Ltd has produced a performance report detailing budgeted and actual cost for last month.

Calculate the amount of the variance for each cost type and then determine whether it is adverse or favourable by putting a tick in the relevant column of the table below.

.

Cost Type	Budget £	Actual £	Variance	Adverse	Favourable
Direct Materials	38,400	40,100	£		
Direct Labour	74,200	73,000	£		
Production Overheads	68,000	72,100	£		
Administration Overheads	52,000	54,900	£		
Selling and Distribution Overheads	43,000	41,900	£		

Task 2.13

The following performance report for this month has been produced for Greenside Ltd as summarised in the table below. Any variance in excess of 10% of budget is thought to be significant and should be reported to the relevant manager for review and appropriate action.

Examine the variances in the table below and indicate whether they are significant or not significant by putting a tick in the relevant column.

✔

Cost Type	Budget	Variance	Adverse/ Favourable	Significant	Not Significant
Direct Materials	£39,000	£3,300	A		
Direct Labour	£75,000	£8,000	A		
Production Overheads	£69,000	£4,200	F		
Administration Overheads	£53,000	£5,900	A		
Selling and Distribution Overheads	£41,000	£2,100	A		

Task 2.14

It was noted from the performance report for Greenside Ltd for an earlier month that the following cost variances were significant:

•   Direct labour costs

•   Administration overheads

These variances needed to be reported to the relevant managers for review and appropriate action if required.

Select from the following list a relevant manager for each significant variance to whom the performance report should be sent:

•   Human resources (HR) manager

•   Production manager

•   Administration manager

Variance	Manager
Direct labour costs	
Administration overheads	

Basic costing

Practice assessment 3

Time allowance: 2 hours

Section 1

Task 1.1

The table below lists some of the characteristics of financial accounting and management accounting systems.

Indicate which characteristics relate to each system by putting a tick in the relevant column of the table below.

✔

Characteristic	Financial Accounting	Management Accounting
One of its main outputs is a summarised historical financial statement that is produced annually		
One of its main purposes is useful information about costs within the organisation		
It can involve making comparisons between actual costs and budgeted costs		
Its output is controlled by legislation and accounting standards		

Task 1.2

Roller Ltd is a manufacturer of garden equipment.

Classify the following costs into materials, labour and overheads by putting a tick in the relevant column of the table below.

✔

Cost	Materials	Labour	Overheads
Steel used to make garden forks			
Insurance of factory			
Wages of production workers			
Machinery maintenance contract			

Task 1.3

Takeit Ltd is in business as a transport (haulage) company.

Classify the following costs by nature (direct or indirect) by putting a tick in the relevant column of the table below.

✔

Cost	Direct	Indirect
Lorry drivers' wages		
Cost of replacement tyres for lorries		
Wages of office administrator		
Motorway toll charges		

Task 1.4

Roller Ltd manufactures garden equipment.

Classify the following costs by function (production, administration, selling and distribution or finance) by putting a tick in the relevant column of the table below.

✔

Cost	Production	Administration	Selling and Distribution	Finance
Purchases of wood for fork handles				
Costs of delivering garden equipment to retail outlets				
Loan interest				
Salaries of Administration Department staff				

Task 1.5

Roller Ltd is a manufacturer of garden equipment.

Classify the following costs by their behaviour (fixed, variable, or semi-variable) by putting a tick in the relevant column of the table below.

✔

Cost	Fixed	Variable	Semi-variable
Wood used to make fork handles			
Pay of Marketing Manager which includes a sales-based bonus			
Broadband costs which do not depend on internet usage			
Loan interest			

Task 1.6

Zoom Ltd operates a garage business which comprises of second hand car sales and vehicle servicing. It uses an alpha-numeric coding structure based on one profit centre and three cost centres as outlined below. Each code has a sub-code so each transaction will be coded as */***

Profit/Cost Centre	Code	Sub-classification	Sub-code
Sales	W	Second Hand Car Sales	100
		Vehicle Servicing Sales	200
Second Hand Cars	X	Direct Cost	100
		Indirect Cost	200
Vehicle Servicing	Y	Direct Cost	100
		Indirect Cost	200
Administration	Z	Direct Cost	100
		Indirect Cost	200

Code the following revenue and cost transactions, which have been extracted from purchase invoices, sales invoices and payroll, using the table below.

Transaction	Code
Revenue from sale of Ford car to Mr Smith	/
Cost of maintenance of electronic diagnostic equipment used for servicing vehicles	/
Revenue from servicing vehicles during April	/
Purchase cost of second hand cars at auction	/
Cost of oil used to service vehicles	/
Cost of wax used to polish cars ready for sale	/

Task 1.7

Roller Limited is a manufacturer of garden equipment and uses a coding system for its elements of cost (materials labour or overhead expenses) and then further classifies each element by nature (direct or indirect cost) as below. So, for example, the code for direct materials is 50/100.

Element of Cost	Code	Nature of Cost	Code
Materials	50	Direct	100
		Indirect	200
Labour	60	Direct	100
		Indirect	200
Overhead Expenses	70	Direct	100
		Indirect	200

Code the following costs, extracted from invoices and payroll, using the table below.

Cost	Code
Wages of production worker	
Wages of delivery driver	
Steel to make garden spades	
Insurance for factory	
Repairs to factory roof	

Task 1.8

Identify the type of cost behaviour (fixed, variable or semi-variable) illustrated by each statement below by putting a tick in the relevant column of the table below.

	Fixed	Variable	Semi-variable
At 500 units, costs total £3,500, and at 1,500 units costs total £10,500			
At 500 units, costs total £6,500, and at 1,500 units costs total £13,500			
At 500 units, costs are £10 per unit, and at 1,000 units costs are £5 per unit			

Task 1.9

Classify the following costs as either fixed or variable by putting a tick in the relevant column of the table below.

✔

Costs	Fixed	Variable
Interest on loan used to purchase factory		
Pay for production workers based on a fixed amount per unit produced		
Salaries of accounts office staff		
Wages of factory cleaning staff based on regular hours		

Task 1.10

Complete the table below showing fixed costs, variable costs, total costs and unit cost at the different levels of production. Carry out unit cost calculations to the nearest penny.

Units	Fixed Costs	Variable Costs	Total Costs	Unit Cost
5,000	£	£	£	£
7,500	£	£	£	£
10,000	£20,000	£50,000	£70,000	£7.00

Task 1.11

Nelson Ltd is costing a single product which has the following cost details for a production level of 25,000 units:

Variable material costs per unit is £15

Labour is a variable cost. It costs £16 per hour. Each unit takes 15 minutes to produce.

Total Fixed Overheads are £50,000

Complete the following total cost and unit cost table for a production level of 25,000 units.

	Total Cost	Unit Cost
Materials	£	£
Labour	£	£
Fixed Overheads	£	£
Total	£	£

Task 1.12

Eureka Ltd makes a single product and for a production level of 20,000 units has the following cost details:

Materials 2,000 kilos at £18 per kilo

Labour 4,000 hours at £12 an hour

Fixed Overheads £60,000

Complete the table below to show the unit cost at the production level of 20,000 units.

	Unit Cost
Materials	£
Labour	£
Overheads	£
Total	£

Section 2

Task 2.1

Reorder the following costs into a manufacturing account format on the right side of the table below.

	£		£
Prime cost	293,000		
Purchases of raw materials	111,000		
Opening inventory of raw materials	23,000		
Closing inventory of finished goods	38,000		
Direct labour	176,000		
Cost of goods manufactured	407,000		
Cost of goods sold	424,000		
Manufacturing cost	419,000		
Direct materials used	117,000		
Opening inventory of work in progress	37,000		
Opening inventory of finished goods	55,000		
Manufacturing overheads	126,000		
Closing inventory of work in progress	49,000		
Closing inventory of raw materials	17,000		

Task 2.2

You are told that the opening inventory of a single raw material in the stores is 800 units at £12 per unit. During the period a receipt of 1,000 units at £11 per units is received, followed by an issue of 1,500 units.

Identify the valuation method described in the statements below.

Statement	FIFO	LIFO	AVCO
The closing inventory is valued at £3,600			
The issue of 1,500 units is costed at £17,300			
The closing inventory is valued at £3,300			

Task 2.3

Identify whether the following statements are true or false by putting a tick in the relevant column of the table below.

	True	False
AVCO values issues at the weighted average cost of the inventory		
FIFO values issues at the most recent purchase price(s)		
LIFO values issues at the most recent purchase price(s)		
FIFO values inventory at the weighted average cost of the inventory		
LIFO values inventory at the most recent purchase price(s)		
FIFO values inventory at the most recent purchase price(s)		

Task 2.4

Nelson Ltd has the following movements in a certain type of inventory into and out of its stores for the month of February:

Date	Receipts		Issues	
	Units	Cost	Units	Cost
February 5	50	£400		
February 9	150	£1,275		
February 13	300	£2,550		
February 18			400	
February 26	250	£2,250		

Complete the table below for the issue and closing inventory values.

Method	Value of Issue on 18 Feb	Inventory at 28 Feb
FIFO	£	£
LIFO	£	£
AVCO	£	£

Task 2.5

Identify the following statements as true or false by putting a tick in the relevant column of the table below.

✔

	True	False
Direct material costs normally behave as variable costs		
Indirect costs cannot be identified specifically with the product made		

Task 2.6

Identify one feature for each labour payment method by putting a tick in the relevant column of the table below.

✔

Payment Method	Time-rate	Piecework	Time-rate plus bonus
All employees earn at least a certain amount, but efficient employees are rewarded with additional amounts			
Efficient employees will earn the same amount as inefficient employees			
An employee's pay would double if his output doubled			

Task 2.7

Categorise the following examples of labour payments by putting a tick in the relevant column of the table below.

✔

Example of Payment	Time-rate	Piecework	Time-rate plus bonus
Payment is at a rate of £10 per hour			
Payment is based on £9 per hour plus £1 for every unit made exceeding 30 per week			
Payment is at a rate of £5 per unit produced			

Task 2.8

Nelson Ltd pays a time-rate of £9 per hour to its direct labour for a standard 38 hour week. Any of the labour force working in excess of 38 hours is paid an overtime rate of £13.50 per hour.

Calculate the gross wage for the week for the two workers in the table below.

Worker	Hours Worked	Basic Wage	Overtime	Gross Wage
M Singh	38 hours	£	£	£
S Spencer	43 hours	£	£	£

Task 2.9

Nelson Ltd uses a piecework method to pay labour in one of its factories. The rate used is £3.09 per unit produced.

Calculate the gross wage for the week for the two workers in the table below.

Worker	Units Produced in Week	Gross Wage
G Purcell	89 units	£
M Katz	103 units	£

Task 2.10

Nelson Ltd uses a time-rate method with bonus to pay its direct labour in one of its factories. The time-rate used is £8.50 per hour and a worker is expected to produce 4 units an hour. Anything over this and the worker is paid a bonus of £1.50 per unit.

Calculate the gross wage for the week including bonus for the three workers in the table below.

Worker	Hours Worked	Units Produced	Basic Wage	Bonus	Gross Wage
J Jarvis	40	150	£	£	£
S Poole	40	185	£	£	£
D Kerr	40	173	£	£	£

Task 2.11

Identify the following statements as being true or false by putting a tick in the relevant column of the table below.

✔

	True	False
A variance can be calculated as the difference between expected and actual cost		
If expected cost is greater than actual cost the variance is favourable		

Task 2.12

Granville Ltd has produced a performance report detailing budgeted and actual cost for last month.

Calculate the amount of the variance for each cost type and then determine whether it is adverse or favourable by putting a tick in the relevant column of the table below.

✔

Cost Type	Budget £	Actual £	Variance	Adverse	Favourable
Direct Materials	53,500	55,100	£		
Direct Labour	79,600	79,000	£		
Production Overheads	55,600	56,200	£		
Administration Overheads	60,200	59,900	£		
Selling and Distribution Overheads	30,900	31,900	£		

Task 2.13

The following performance report for this month has been produced for Granville Ltd as summarised in the table below. Any variance in excess of 4.5% of budget is thought to be significant and should be reported to the relevant manager for review and appropriate action.

Examine the adverse (A) and favourable (F) variances in the table below and calculate the actual costs. Indicate whether each variance is significant or not significant by putting a tick in the relevant column.

✔

Cost Type	Budget £	Variance £	Actual Cost £	Significant	Not Significant
Direct Materials	47,000	2,300 A			
Direct Labour	65,000	2,150 A			
Production Overheads	73,000	3,200 F			
Administration Overheads	35,000	900 F			
Selling and Distribution Overheads	37,500	1,680 A			

Task 2.14

It was noted from the performance report for Nelson Ltd for an earlier month that the following cost variances were significant:

• Administration overheads cost

• Selling and distribution overheads cost

These variances needed to be reported to the relevant managers for review and appropriate action if required.

Select from the following list a relevant manager for each significant variance to whom the performance report should be sent:

• Purchasing manager

• Training manager

• Sales manager

• Production manager

• Administration manager

• Transport manager

Variance	Manager
Administration overheads cost	
Selling and distribution overheads cost	

Practice assessment answers

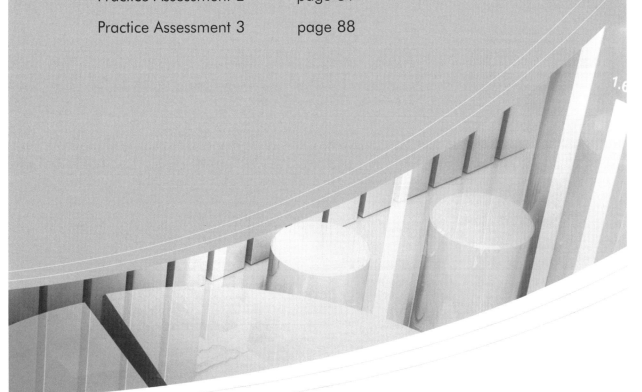

Section 1

Task 1.1

Characteristic	Financial Accounting	Management Accounting
It is concerned with recording historic costs and revenues	✔	
One of its main purposes is to provide information for annual financial statements	✔	
It is accurate, with no use of estimates	✔	
It looks forward to show what is likely to happen in the future		✔

Task 1.2

Cost	Materials	Labour	Overheads
Meat used in burgers	✔		
Electricity used in factory			✔
Boxes to pack burgers	✔		
Expenses of the sales manager			✔

Task 1.3

Cost	Direct	Indirect
Fuel for taxis	✔	
Cost of servicing taxis		✔
Wages of taxi drivers	✔	
Wages of reception staff		✔

Task 1.4

Cost	Production	Administration	Selling and Distribution
Purchases of components for mobile telephones	✔		
Commission paid to sales staff			✔
Rent of offices		✔	
Wages of staff who assemble telephones	✔		

Task 1.5

Cost	Fixed	Variable	Semi-Variable
Labour costs paid on a time basis	✔		
Maintenance of website	✔		
Power costs which include a standing charge			✔
Packing materials for completed instruments		✔	

Task 1.6

Transaction	Code
Factory lighting	B/200
Repairs to warehouse	D/200
Meat for making burgers	B/100
Sales to 'Kings Restaurant'	A/100
Commission to sales staff	D/200
Stationery for Administration	C/200

Task 1.7

Cost	Code
Wages of taxi driver	60/100
Vehicle insurance for taxis	70/200
Wages of reception staff	60/200
Fuel for taxis	50/100
Office rent	70/200

Task 1.8

	True	False
Variable costs change in proportion to changes in activity level	✔	
Fixed costs remain unchanged when activity levels change	✔	
Semi-variable costs change in proportion to changes in activity level		✔

Task 1.9

Cost	Fixed	Variable
Factory insurance	✔	
Bonus for production staff paid per item produced		✔
Salaries of administration staff	✔	
Repairs to a factory used for production	✔	

Task 1.10

Units	Fixed Costs	Variable Costs	Total Costs	Unit Cost
5,000	£25,000	£10,000	£35,000	£7.00
7,500	£25,000	£15,000	£40,000	£5.33
10,000	£25,000	£20,000	£45,000	£4.50
12,500	£25,000	£25,000	£50,000	£4.00

Task 1.11

	Total Cost	Unit Cost
Materials	£96,000	£8
Labour	£60,000	£5
Fixed Overheads	£48,000	£4
Total	£204,000	£17

Task 1.12

Element	Unit Cost
Materials	£3.00
Labour	£2.75
Overheads	£4.00
Total	£9.75

Section 2

Task 2.1

	£		£
Closing inventory of raw materials	10,000	Opening inventory of raw materials	9,000
Direct labour	86,000	Purchases of raw materials	48,000
Opening inventory of raw materials	9,000	Closing inventory of raw materials	10,000
Closing inventory of finished goods	25,000	Direct materials used	47,000
Prime cost	133,000	Direct labour	86,000
Factory cost of goods manufactured	195,000	Prime cost	133,000
Cost of goods sold	200,000	Manufacturing overheads	64,000
Factory cost	197,000	Factory cost	197,000
Purchases of raw materials	48,000	Opening inventory of work in progress	9,000
Opening inventory of work in progress	9,000	Closing inventory of work in progress	11,000
Opening inventory of finished goods	30,000	Factory cost of goods manufactured	195,000
Manufacturing overheads	64,000	Opening inventory of finished goods	30,000
Direct materials used	47,000	Closing inventory of finished goods	25,000
Closing inventory of work in progress	11,000	Cost of goods sold	200,000

Task 2.2

Characteristic	FIFO	LIFO	AVCO
Inventory is valued at the most recent purchase cost	✔		
Issues are valued at the average of the cost of purchases			✔
Issues are valued at the oldest relevant purchase cost	✔		

Task 2.3

	True	False
AVCO costs issues of inventory at the most recent purchase price		✔
FIFO costs issues of inventory at the oldest relevant purchase price	✔	
LIFO costs issues of inventory at the oldest relevant purchase price		✔
FIFO values closing inventory at the most recent purchase price	✔	
LIFO values closing inventory at the most recent purchase price		✔
AVCO values closing inventory at the most recent purchase price		✔

Task 2.4

Method	Value of Issue on 18 August	Inventory at 31 August
FIFO	£3,695	£2,505
LIFO	£3,760	£2,440
AVCO	£3,722	£2,478

Task 2.5

	True	False
Direct material costs cannot be identified with the goods being made or the service being produced		✔
Indirect costs never change when the level of activity alters		✔

Task 2.6

Payment Method	Time-rate	Piecework	Time-rate plus bonus
Labour is paid based entirely on attendance at the workplace	✔		
Labour is paid a basic rate plus an extra amount if an agreed level of production is exceeded			✔
Labour is paid entirely according to each individual's output		✔	

Task 2.7

Payment Method	Time-rate	Piecework	Time-rate plus bonus
Employee knows that pay will not fall below certain amount but will increase if output is high			✔
Employer and employee can both plan for regular expected amounts	✔		
Employer's labour cost is entirely proportional to output		✔	

Task 2.8

Worker	Hours Worked	Basic Wage	Overtime	Gross Wage
A Smith	37 hours	£296.00	£0.00	£296.00
S Collins	41 hours	£296.00	£64.00	£360.00

Task 2.9

Worker	Units Produced in Week	Gross Wage
G Powell	109 units	£235.44
S Singh	123 units	£265.68

Task 2.10

Worker	Hours Worked	Units Produced	Basic Wage	Bonus	Gross Wage
A Weaton	40	250	£400.00	£0.00	£400.00
J Davis	40	295	£400.00	£7.50	£407.50
M Laston	40	280	£400.00	£0.00	£400.00

Task 2.11

	True	False
A variance can be calculated as the difference between expected and actual income	✔	
If expected income is greater than actual income the variance is favourable		✔

Task 2.12

Cost Type	Budget £	Actual £	Variance	Adverse	Favourable
Direct Materials	34,500	38,100	£3,600	✔	
Direct Labour	71,300	70,000	£1,300		✔
Production Overheads	48,600	49,100	£500	✔	
Administration Overheads	89,400	84,900	£4,500		✔
Selling and Distribution Overheads	51,200	51,900	£700	✔	

Task 2.13

Cost Type	Budget	Variance	Adverse/ Favourable	Significant	Not Significant
Direct Materials	£38,000	£3,300	A	✔	
Direct Labour	£71,000	£8,000	A	✔	
Production Overheads	£43,000	£4,200	F	✔	
Administration Overheads	£50,000	£2,900	A		✔
Selling and Distribution Overheads	£47,000	£2,100	A		✔

Task 2.14

Variance	Manager
Production overheads cost	Production manager
Direct materials cost	Purchasing manager or Production manager

Practice Assessment 2

Section 1

Task 1.1

Characteristic	Financial Accounting	Management Accounting
It is based on past events	✔	
Its purpose is to provide information for managers		✔
It is based on future events		✔
It complies with company law and accounting rules	✔	

Task 1.2

Cost	Materials	Labour	Overheads
Wood used in garden chairs	✔		
Rent of factory			✔
Wages of carpenters in the cutting department		✔	
Expenses of the office manager			✔

Task 1.3

Cost	Direct	Indirect
Conditioner used on hair	✔	
Insurance of salon		✔
Wages of salon cleaner		✔
Wages of hair stylists	✔	

Task 1.4

Cost	Production	Administration	Selling and Distribution
Purchases of sugar	✔		
Depreciation of sales department's motor vehicles			✔
Insurance of office furniture		✔	
Salaries of production workers	✔		

Task 1.5

Cost	Fixed	Variable	Semi-Variable
Material used in the production process		✔	
Advertising budget for the year	✔		
Electricity costs which include a standing charge			✔
Labour costs paid on a piecework basis		✔	

Task 1.6

Transaction	Code
Office heating	300/200
Warehouse rent	400/200
Sales to Oxford, UK	100/100
Sales to North America	100/200
Materials to stain tables	200/100
Factory canteen wages	200/200

Task 1.7

Cost	Code
Salary of trainee hairdresser	B100
Legal costs to renew lease of salon	C200
Wages of salon cleaner	B200
Cleaning materials used by cleaner	A200
Colouring materials used on customers	A100

Task 1.8

	True	False
Variable costs change directly with changes in activity	✔	
Fixed costs change directly with changes in activity		✔
Semi-variable costs have a fixed and variable element	✔	

Task 1.9

Cost	Fixed	Variable
Direct materials		✔
Wages of production workers paid using a time-rate method	✔	
Wages of production workers paid by a piecework method		✔
Rent for a factory used for production	✔	

Task 1.10

Units	Fixed Costs	Variable Costs	Total Costs	Unit Cost
1,000	£12,000	£3,000	£15,000	£15.00
2,000	£12,000	£6,000	£18,000	£9.00
3,000	£12,000	£9,000	£21,000	£7.00
4,000	£12,000	£12,000	£24,000	£6.00

Task 1.11

Element	Total Cost	Unit Cost
Materials	£40,000	£2.00
Labour	£60,000	£3.00
Fixed costs	£80,000	£4.00
Total	£180,000	£9.00

Task 1.12

Element	Unit Cost
Materials	£5.00
Labour	£4.00
Expenses	£2.00
Total	£11.00

Section 2

Task 2.1

	£		£
Closing Inventory of Work in Progress	10,000	Opening Inventory of Raw Materials	7,000
Direct Labour	97,000	Purchases of Raw Materials	50,000
Opening Inventory of Raw Materials	7,000	Closing Inventory of Raw Materials	10,000
Closing Inventory of Finished Goods	25,000	Direct materials used	47,000
Closing Inventory of Raw Materials	10,000	Direct Labour	97,000
Manufacturing Overheads	53,000	Prime cost	144,000
Cost of goods sold	200,000	Manufacturing Overheads	53,000
Factory cost	197,000	Factory cost	197,000
Purchases of Raw Materials	50,000	Opening Inventory of Work in Progress	8,000
Opening Inventory of Work in Progress	8,000	Closing Inventory of Work in Progress	10,000
Opening Inventory of Finished Goods	30,000	Factory cost of goods manufactured	195,000
Prime cost	144,000	Opening Inventory of Finished Goods	30,000
Direct materials used	47,000	Closing Inventory of Finished Goods	25,000
Factory cost of goods manufactured	195,000	Cost of goods sold	200,000

Task 2.2

Characteristic	FIFO	LIFO	AVCO
Issues are valued at the most recent purchase cost		✔	
Inventory is valued at the average of the cost of purchases			✔
Inventory is valued at the most recent purchase cost	✔		

Task 2.3

	True	False
FIFO costs issues of inventory at the most recent purchase price		✔
AVCO costs issues of inventory at the oldest purchase price		✔
LIFO costs issues of inventory at the oldest purchase price		✔
FIFO values closing inventory at the most recent purchase price	✔	
LIFO values closing inventory at the most recent purchase price		✔
AVCO values closing inventory at the latest purchase price		✔

Task 2.4

Method	Value of Issue on 18 March	Inventory at 31 March
FIFO	£2,300	£4,400
LIFO	£2,900	£3,800
AVCO	£2,580	£4,120

Task 2.5

	True	False
Direct labour costs can be identified with the goods being made or the service being produced	✔	
Indirect costs vary directly with the level of activity		✔

Task 2.6

Payment Method	Time-rate	Piecework	Time-rate plus bonus
Labour is paid based entirely on the production achieved		✔	
Labour is paid extra if an agreed level of output is exceeded			✔
Labour is paid according to hours worked	✔		

Task 2.7

Payment Method	Time-rate	Piecework	Time-rate plus bonus
Assured level of remuneration for employee, but no reward for working efficiently	✔		
Employee earnings depend entirely on output		✔	
Assured level of remuneration and reward for working efficiently			✔

Task 2.8

Worker	Hours Worked	Basic Wage	Overtime	Gross Wage
A Singh	35 hours	£350.00	£0.00	£350.00
S Callaghan	40 hours	£350.00	£75.00	£425.00

Task 2.9

Worker	Units Produced in Week	Gross Wage
G Patel	300 units	£240.00
A Jones	400 units	£320.00

Task 2.10

Worker	Hours Worked	Units Produced	Basic Wage	Bonus	Gross Wage
A Smith	35	150	£420.00	£0.00	£420.00
J O'Hara	35	175	£420.00	£0.00	£420.00
M Stizgt	35	210	£420.00	£35.00	£455.00

Task 2.11

	True	False
A variance is the difference between budgeted and actual cost	✔	
A favourable variance means budgeted costs are greater than actual costs	✔	

Task 2.12

Cost Type	Budget £	Actual £	Variance	Adverse	Favourable
Direct Materials	38,400	40,100	£1,700	✔	
Direct Labour	74,200	73,000	£1,200		✔
Production Overheads	68,000	72,100	£4,100	✔	
Administration Overheads	52,000	54,900	£2,900	✔	
Selling and Distribution Overheads	43,000	41,900	£1,100		✔

Task 2.13

Cost Type	Budget	Variance	Adverse/ Favourable	Significant	Not Significant
Direct Materials	£39,000	£3,300	A		✔
Direct Labour	£75,000	£8,000	A	✔	
Production Overheads	£69,000	£4,200	F		✔
Administration Overheads	£53,000	£5,900	A	✔	
Selling and Distribution Overheads	£41,000	£2,100	A		✔

Task 2.14

Variance	Manager
Direct labour costs	HR Manager or Production Manager
Administration overheads	Administration Manager

Practice Assessment 3

Section 1

Task 1.1

Characteristic	Financial Accounting	Management Accounting
One of its main outputs is a summarised historical financial statement that is produced annually	✔	
One of its main purposes is useful information about costs within the organisation		✔
It can involve making comparisons between actual costs and budgeted costs		✔
Its output is controlled by legislation and accounting standards	✔	

Task 1.2

Cost	Materials	Labour	Overheads
Steel used to make garden forks	✔		
Insurance of factory			✔
Wages of production workers		✔	
Machinery maintenance contract			✔

Task 1.3

Cost	Direct	Indirect
Lorry drivers' wages	✔	
Cost of replacement tyres for lorries		✔
Wages of office administrator		✔
Motorway toll charges	✔	

Task 1.4

Cost	Production	Administration	Selling and Distribution	Finance
Purchases of wood for fork handles	✔			
Costs of delivering garden equipment to retail outlets			✔	
Loan interest				✔
Salaries of Administration Department staff		✔		

Task 1.5

Cost	Fixed	Variable	Semi-variable
Wood used to make fork handles		✔	
Pay of Marketing Manager which includes a sales-based bonus			✔
Broadband costs which do not depend on internet usage	✔		
Loan interest	✔		

Task 1.6

Transaction	Code
Revenue from sale of Ford car to Mr Smith	W/100
Cost of maintenance of electronic diagnostic equipment used for servicing vehicles	Y/200
Revenue from servicing vehicles during April	W/200
Purchase cost of second hand cars at auction	X/100
Cost of oil used to service vehicles	Y/100
Cost of wax used to polish cars ready for sale	X/200

Task 1.7

Cost	Code
Wages of production worker	60/100
Wages of delivery driver	60/200
Steel to make garden spades	50/100
Insurance for factory	70/200
Repairs to factory roof	70/200

Task 1.8

	Fixed	Variable	Semi-variable
At 500 units, costs total £3,500, and at 1,500 units costs total £10,500		✔	
At 500 units, costs total £6,500, and at 1,500 units costs total £13,500			✔
At 500 units, costs are £10 per unit, and at 1,000 units costs are £5 per unit	✔		

Task 1.9

Costs	Fixed	Variable
Interest on loan used to purchase factory	✔	
Pay for production workers based on a fixed amount per unit produced		✔
Salaries of accounts office staff	✔	
Wages of factory cleaning staff based on regular hours	✔	

Task 1.10

Units	Fixed Costs	Variable Costs	Total Costs	Unit Cost
5,000	£20,000	£25,000	£45,000	£9.00
7,500	£20,000	£37,500	£57,500	£7.67
10,000	£20,000	£50,000	£70,000	£7.00

Task 1.11

	Total Cost	Unit Cost
Materials	£375,000	£15.00
Labour	£100,000	£4.00
Fixed Overheads	£50,000	£2.00
Total	£525,000	£21.00

Task 1.12

	Unit Cost
Materials	£1.80
Labour	£2.40
Overheads	£3.00
Total	£7.20

Section 2

Task 2.1

	£
Opening inventory of raw materials	23,000
Purchases of raw materials	111,000
Closing inventory of raw materials	17,000
Direct materials used	117,000
Direct labour	176,000
Prime cost	293,000
Manufacturing overheads	126,000
Manufacturing cost	419,000
Opening inventory of work in progress	37,000
Closing inventory of work in progress	49,000
Cost of goods manufactured	407,000
Opening inventory of finished goods	55,000
Closing inventory of finished goods	38,000
Cost of goods sold	424,000

Task 2.2

Statement	FIFO	LIFO	AVCO
The closing inventory is valued at £3,600		✔	
The issue of 1,500 units is costed at £17,300	✔		
The closing inventory is valued at £3,300	✔		

Task 2.3

	True	False
AVCO values issues at the weighted average cost of the inventory	✔	
FIFO values issues at the most recent purchase price(s)		✔
LIFO values issues at the most recent purchase price(s)	✔	
FIFO values inventory at the weighted average cost of the inventory		✔
LIFO values inventory at the most recent purchase price(s)		✔
FIFO values inventory at the most recent purchase price(s)	✔	

Task 2.4

Method	Value of Issue on 18 Feb	Inventory at 28 Feb
FIFO	£3,375	£3,100
LIFO	£3,400	£3,075
AVCO	£3,380	£3,095

Task 2.5

	True	False
Direct material costs normally behave as variable costs	✔	
Indirect costs cannot be identified specifically with the product made	✔	

Task 2.6

Payment Method	Time-rate	Piecework	Time-rate plus bonus
All employees earn at least a certain amount, but efficient employees are rewarded with additional amounts			✔
Efficient employees will earn the same amount as inefficient employees	✔		
An employee's pay would double if his output doubled		✔	

Task 2.7

Example of Payment	Time-rate	Piecework	Time-rate plus bonus
Payment is at a rate of £10 per hour	✔		
Payment is based on £9 per hour plus £1 for every unit made exceeding 30 per week			✔
Payment is at a rate of £5 per unit produced		✔	

Task 2.8

Worker	Hours Worked	Basic Wage	Overtime	Gross Wage
M Singh	38 hours	£342.00	£0.00	£342.00
S Spencer	43 hours	£342.00	£67.50	£409.50

Task 2.9

Worker	Units Produced in Week	Gross Wage
G Purcell	89 units	£275.01
M Katz	103 units	£318.27

Task 2.10

Worker	Hours Worked	Units Produced	Basic Wage	Bonus	Gross Wage
J Jarvis	40	150	£340.00	£0.00	£340.00
S Poole	40	185	£340.00	£37.50	£377.50
D Kerr	40	173	£340.00	£19.50	£359.50

Task 2.11

	True	False
A variance can be calculated as the difference between expected and actual cost	✔	
If expected cost is greater than actual cost the variance is favourable	✔	

Task 2.12

Cost Type	Budget £	Actual £	Variance	Adverse	Favourable
Direct Materials	53,500	55,100	£1,600	✔	
Direct Labour	79,600	79,000	£600		✔
Production Overheads	55,600	56,200	£600	✔	
Administration Overheads	60,200	59,900	£300		✔
Selling and Distribution Overheads	30,900	31,900	£1,000	✔	

Task 2.13

Cost Type	Budget £	Variance £	Actual Cost £	Significant	Not Significant
Direct Materials	47,000	2,300 A	49,300	✔	
Direct Labour	65,000	2,150 A	67,150		✔
Production Overheads	73,000	3,200 F	69,800		✔
Administration Overheads	35,000	900 F	34,100		✔
Selling and Distribution Overheads	37,500	1,680 A	39,180		✔

Task 2.14

Variance	Manager
Administration overheads cost	Administration manager
Selling and distribution overheads cost	Sales manager or Transport manager